DATE DUE

FEB 19 02			

Taking Your Camera to

SPAIN

Ted Park

Raintree Steck-Vaughn Publishers

A Harcourt Company

Austin · New York
www.steck-vaughn.com

Published by Raintree Steck-Vaughn Publishers,
an imprint of Steck-Vaughn Company

Library of Congress Cataloging-in-Publication Data
Park, Ted
    Spain / by Ted Park.
        p. cm. — (Taking your camera to)
    Includes index.
    ISBN 0-7398-1809-0
    1. Spain—Juvenile literature. [1. Spain.] I. Title. II. Series.

DP17 .P35 2000
946—dc21   00-041031

Printed in the United States of America
10 9 8 7 6 5 4 3 2 1 W 04 03 02 01

Photo acknowledgments
Cover ©Travelpix/FPG International; pp.1, 3a, 3b ©Superstock; p.3c ©Marco Corsetti/FPG International; pp.3d, 4, 5, 8 ©Superstock; p.9 ©Travel Pix/FPG International; p.11 ©Superstock; p.13 ©Jim Cummins/FPG Internatioanl; p.14 ©Jose Luis Banus/FPG International; p.15 ©Marco Corsetti/FPG International; p.16 ©Superstock; p.17 ©Spencer Grant/FPG International; p.19 ©Superstock; p.20 ©Travel Pix/FPG International; p.23 ©Reuters New Media Inc./CORBIS; pp.25a, 25b, 27 ©Superstock; p.28a ©Travel Pix/FPG International; p.28b ©Jim Cummins/FPG Internatioanl; pp.29a, 29b ©Superstock.

All statistics in the Quick Facts section come from *The New York Times Almanac* (2000) and *The World Almanac* (2000)

Contents

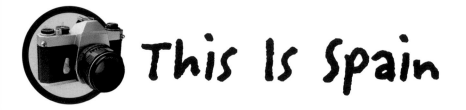 # This Is Spain

Spain is a large country in southwestern Europe. In the north, there are many tall mountains. In the middle of the country there is a huge, dry plateau. A plateau is a flat area of land that is higher than the land around it. This plateau is called the Meseta. This is the Spanish word for "plateau." Along the south coast there are

Seville at night

Many tourists visit the Canary Islands beaches.

sandy beaches. If you took your camera to Spain, you could take photographs of many things.

Spain has many interesting cities. Two of the largest are Madrid and Barcelona. Seville is in the southwest. It has a famous building called the Tower of Gold. Its name comes from the golden tiles that covered the walls around the city. Valencia is a port on the Mediterranean Sea.

Spain also has beautiful countryside. There you can see orange and olive trees growing.

This book will show you some of these places. It will also tell you much about the country of Spain. If you learn about Spain before you take your camera there, you will enjoy your visit more.

5 📷

# The Place

Spain is the third largest country in Europe. It is almost square in shape. The country is about 590 miles (950 km) from north to south. It is about 675 miles (1,085 km) from east to west. Spain is about twice the size of the state of Oregon.

The Atlantic Ocean is on the northwestern side of Spain. The Mediterranean Sea is on the southeastern side. The Pyrenees Mountains in the northeast divide Spain and France. These mountains are about 280 miles (450 km) long. Spain has more mountains than any other country in Europe except Switzerland.

Portugal borders Spain in the west. Together Spain and Portugal make up the Iberian Peninsula. A peninsula is a piece of land surrounded on three sides by water.

Two groups of islands belong to Spain. One is the Balearics, which is made up of five islands. They are in the Mediterranean Sea. The other group of islands is the Canary Islands. They are in the Atlantic Ocean, very close to Africa. The Canary Islands are made up of seven islands.

7

The Pyrenees Mountains are in northeastern Spain.

Gibraltar is a small piece of land in the south that separates Spain from Africa. It is just 3 square miles (6.5 sq km) in size and only 8 miles (13 km) wide at its thinnest point. Gibraltar belongs to Great Britain.

Much of the land that faces the Atlantic Ocean is covered with forests. Not many people live there. This is where most of Spain's mountains are located. Along the Mediterranean Sea there are many sandy beaches and vacation places. This part of Spain includes the popular beaches of the Costa del Sol, which means "Coast of the Sun."

 8

The weather in northern Spain is cool and wet. There is usually rain in the winter and sometimes in the summer. Along the Mediterranean Sea the climate is warm and sunny much of the year.

Spain's longest river is the Tagus, which is the river's name in Portuguese. The river runs through both Spain and Portugal. In Spanish its name is Tajo. Spain's second longest river is the Ebro, which flows into the Mediterranean Sea. All of Spain's other main rivers flow into the Atlantic Ocean.

Gibraltar is on the Mediterranean Sea.

Madrid

Madrid became the capital of Spain in 1561. The city was chosen because it is in the center of the country. Madrid is in the region of Castile. Regions are like states.

Madrid sits on a plateau that is 2,100 feet (640 m) high. The city has very hot summers and very cold, but dry, winters. Most days are sunny, which allow the people of Madrid to enjoy outdoor cafés and restaurants.

Madrid is a modern city. More than 4 million people live there. Madrid has broad avenues lined with modern office buildings. There are also many old buildings in Madrid. One of them is the Royal Palace. It was built in the 18th century. It has 2,800 rooms. This makes it one of the world's largest palaces. Today the Royal Palace is a museum.

Madrid is also the home of one of the world's largest art museums, the Prado. The city has a famous flea market. It is called the Rastro.

Spanish TV, newspapers, and many international companies are based in Madrid. Recently the clothing

 10

and leather industry has become big in Madrid. So has the fashion industry.

Because Madrid is in the center of the country, it has become the country's major railroad hub.

If you took your camera on the streets of Madrid, you could photograph all sorts of sights.

Plaza Mayor in Madrid

Places to Visit

Spain has about 10,000 caves in its mountain areas. Famous caves called the Altamira caves are near the city of Santander in the north. In 1879 a young girl went to the caves with her father. Inside the caves she noticed paintings of animals that experts think are about 15,000 years old.

The Alhambra is a palace and fort in Granada. These buildings were built by the Moors, people from North Africa who conquered Spain in A.D. 711. Moorish kings lived in the Alhambra for more than 200 years.

Barcelona is the second largest city in Spain. It is one of the country's main ports. Antonio Gaudí, a famous designer of buildings, lived in Barcelona. His best known work is the church of the Sagrada Familia in Barcelona. This means "holy family" in English. The cathedral was begun in 1884, but it still has not been finished.

The Alhambra has stone carvings that are so fine
that they look like lace.

13 📷

The People

   More than 39 million people live in Spain. About
5,000 years ago, a people known as Iberians lived there.
Over time, groups of people from other parts of
Europe came to Spain. More than 1,200 years ago,
Moors came from North Africa.

   The official language of Spain is a type of Spanish called
Castilian. But people in different parts of the country
pronounce the words differently. Many places in Spain

One fourth of Spanish people are under the age of 16.

Many of the Spanish who live in the countryside are older people.

have their own language as well as Castilian Spanish. In the area of Catalonia, many people speak Catalan. This is similar to the language spoken by people of southern France. Catalan Spanish is spoken in Barcelona.

In the Basque area, some people speak Basque. This is one of the oldest languages in Europe. It is not like any other language in the world. Basques were living in the mountains of northern Spain long before Spain became a country.

15 📷

Life in Spain

Almost half of the population of Spain lives on about 15 percent of the land. Many people are moving from the country to the cities to look for work. They are also going to vacation places on the south coast for the same reason. Most of the people who move to the cities are young.

People often dance a well-known Spanish dance called the flamenco during special holidays.

In some parts of Spain, people still ride horses to get places.

The family is at the center of Spanish life. Until recently, many mothers did not work. They stayed at home to take care of their children. Now families are smaller. Many mothers take jobs to help earn money. However, fewer women in Spain work than in most other European countries.

In Spain, dinner often does not begin until 9:30 or 10:00 P. M. This is because much of Spain is hot. People take a long break during the hottest part of the day. This is known as a siesta. Then people go back to work around 5:00 P. M. Sometimes, in the evenings, when the weather has cooled down, people in the cities take a walk along the main streets or in the squares. This walk is known as the paseo. Then people have dinner.

17 📷

Government and Religion

Spain is a parliamentary monarchy. This means that a monarch, or king or queen, is the head of state. However, it is parliament that makes the laws. The parliament is called the Cortes. The Cortes is made up of the Congress of Deputies and the Senate. The head of the Cortes is the prime minister. The citizens of Spain elect these people. They are elected for four years.

Most Spaniards are Roman Catholics. A few Muslims, Protestants, and Jews live in Spain, but there are not very many. The second-largest cathedral, or big church, in the world is in Spain. It is called Santa Maria, and it is in Seville. It was built between 1402 and 1506. The church is 413 feet (125.8 m) long and 269 feet (82 m) wide.

The Cathedral of Santiago de Compostela in Santiago

18

Earning a Living

There are many ways in Spain for people to earn a living. Farming takes place in much of Spain, but especially in the north. Sheep, cows, and goats are raised there. Farmers grow cereal crops such as wheat and barley in the Meseta. Oxen pull plows. But in the warmer south, more and more farmers are using

Because Spain is surrounded by so much water, fishing is important.

machines. Farmers grow fruits and vegetables in the warm south. Grapes that are made into wine are also grown in Spain. Olives are another important food crop. Some of the olives are exported, or sent out of the country to be sold. Many are made into olive oil.

Spain has few natural resources. Natural resources are things from nature that are useful to people. Two natural resources that Spain has are fossil fuels and minerals. Coal and iron ore are found in the north. Most raw materials are brought, or imported, into Spain. This includes oil. Most of the oil is used for energy.

People cut down trees in the past, but this has stopped. Many new trees have been planted in the last 20 years. Now Spain has more acres of forest than any other country in Europe.

The fishing industry is important. Tourism is also important. More than 50 million visitors a year come to Spain. This is larger than Spain's population. With so many people coming to Spain, larger airports need to be built. This will make jobs. Because so many people visit Spain, the craft industry has grown. Many visitors want to take reminders of their trip home when they leave the country.

School and Sports

In Spain, children have to go to school when they are six years old. The school day starts early and finishes late. Students take a break during the middle of the day, when it is very hot. At the age of 16, students who pass an exam can start taking classes before going to college. Some colleges in Spain are more than 800 years old. The University of Madrid has more than 100,000 students.

Soccer is Spain's most popular sport. It is known by its Spanish name, fútbol. Pelota is a fast-moving Basque ball game. It is played on an indoor court.

Bicycling and hiking are also popular. Along the southern coast Spaniards like to swim and dive.

Bullfighting is a famous Spanish sport. Bullfights are called corridas. Many people around the world dislike these events because of the cruelty shown to the animals. Despite this, bullfights are still popular in Spain.

Soccer is a fast-moving sport.

Food and Holidays

Fish is a popular food. Spaniards eat at least twice as much fish each year as most other Europeans. Other popular foods are sausages, ham, and cheese.

One of Spain's most popular dishes is paella. This is a kind of stew. It is made of fish, seafood, meat, and rice in a rich broth. Meals may be finished with flan, a cooked custard, or with locally grown fruit.

Because most Spaniards are Roman Catholics, most holidays are religious ones. One of the best known is Holy Week. It is called Semana Santa in Spanish. This is the week before Easter. During this time, there are many religious parades.

Some Spanish festivals, or fiestas, may last as long as a week. Many Spaniards celebrate grape harvests with parades. These usually take place in October. In Pamplona, a city in northern Spain, there is a fiesta in which bulls are allowed to run through the streets.

Christmas in Valencia

A tomato festival

# The Future

When you go to Spain, you will see a country that is changing. Many new things are happening there. Today, electronics, chemicals, and computers are important industries. They bring money into the country. They also make jobs for many people.

However, like other nations, Spain has some problems. Many of the roads in Spain are new and large. One fourth of all Spaniards own cars. This means there is a lot of traffic. This is especially true in the summer. This is the time when tourists crowd the roads.

In Spain, there has been some damage to nature. This has happened mainly in the cities and the tourist places. To make sure there are animals and plants in the future, people in Spain have set up many national parks. Different kinds of animals and plants live there safely.

The Spaniards are proud of their country. When you leave Spain, a Spaniard might say "Hasta la vista" to you. This is Spanish for "See you later."

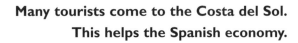
**Many tourists come to the Costa del Sol.
This helps the Spanish economy.**

Quick Facts About
SPAIN

Capital
Madrid

Borders
France, Morocco, Portugal

Area
194,884 square miles
(504,750 sq km)

Population
39.2 million

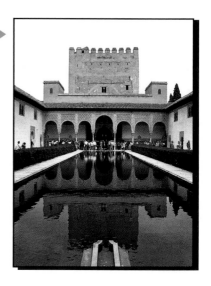

Largest cities
Madrid (2,984,576 people);
Barcelona (1,653,175 people);
Valencia (777,427 people)

Chief crops
grains, vegetables, olives, grapes,
sugar beets, citrus, beef, pork,
poultry, dairy products, fish

Natural resources
coal, lignite, iron ore, uranium,
mercury

Longest river
Tajo, at 626 miles (1,007 km)

28

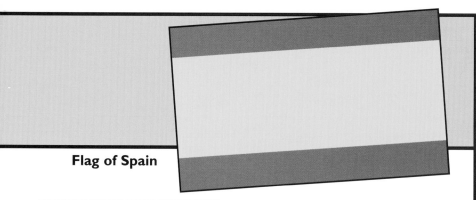

Flag of Spain

Coastline
3,085 miles (4,964 km)

Monetary unit
peseta

Literacy rate
97 percent of the Spanish can read and write.

Major industries
machinery, metals, textiles, shoes, vehicles, processed food, tourism

29

Glossary

Alhambra (al-HAM-bruh) A castle and fort in southern Spain famous for its fine stone carvings

Altamira caves (ahl-tuh-MIR-uh) Famous caves in the mountains of northern Spain that have 15,000-year-old paintings inside them

Barcelona (bahr-suh-LOW-nuh) The second largest city in Spain and one of the country's main ports, located in northeastern Spain

Basque (BASK) The type of Spanish spoken in the Basque area of northern Spain.

Castilian Spanish (kah-STILL-yun) The official language of Spain

Catalan (KAH-tuh-luhn) The type of Spanish spoken in the area of Catalonia, in northeastern Spain

Corridas (ko-REE-thu) The Spanish word for "bullfights"

Cortes (kor-TEZ) The name of Spain's parliament

Fiesta (fee-ES-tuh) A festival

Fútbol (FUT-bahl) The Spanish word for "soccer"

Iberians (eye-BEER-ee-uhnz) People who lived in Spain about 5,000 years ago

Madrid (muh-DRID) The capital of Spain

Meseta (muh-SEH-tuh) The name of the huge, dry plateau in the center of Spain.

Paella (pah-AY-yuh) A stew made of fish, seafood, meat, and rice in a rich broth

Pamplona (pam-PLO-nuh) A city in northern Spain

Parliamentary monarchy (PAR-luh-MEN-tuh-ree MAH-nur-kee) A form of government in which a king or queen is the head of the country but a parliament does the work of governing

Parliament (PAR-luh-munt) The group of people who make the laws in Spain

Paseo (puh-SAY-oh) An unhurried walk

Pelota (puh-LOW-tuh) A fast-moving Basque ball game played on an indoor court

Royal Palace A 2,800-room palace in Madrid that is now a museum

Seville (suh-VIL) A city in southwestern Spain

Siesta (see-ES-tuh) A long break taken during the afternoon

Valencia (vuh-LEN-see-uh) A Spanish port on the Mediterranean Sea

Index